SELF-
HELP
WITHOUT
THE
HYPE

Robert Epstein, Ph.D.

PERFORMANCE
MANAGEMENT
PUBLICATIONS

Published by Performance Management Publications,
A division of Aubrey Daniels & Associates, Inc.
3531 Habersham at Northlake
Tucker, Georgia 30084
(770) 493-5080

Library of Congress Catalog Card
Number: 82-061868
International Standard Book Number: 0-937100-00-5
Printed in the United States of America
1 2 3 4 5 6 7 8 9 - 99 98 97 96

Printed in the United States of America
by DVC Industries

Administrative: Brenda Jernigan, Sandy Stewart
Production Coordinator: Laura-Lee Daniels
Cover Designer: Kevin Hopson

If you wish to be happy for one
hour, get intoxicated.

If you wish to be happy for three
days, get married.

If you wish to be happy for eight
days, kill your pig and eat it.

If you wish to be happy forever,
learn to fish.

—Ancient Chinese Proverb

CONTENTS

To my parents.

INTRODUCTION

This book uses an age-old story format — the Quest — to teach you some practical methods for changing your life. Like Siddhartha, the restless young man in Hermann Hesse's novel, the protagonist in this book is dissatisfied with his life, and he finds a wise old teacher to help him. Siddhartha acquired a very illusive kind of wisdom, so illusive that he couldn't teach it to his own son. Unlike Siddhartha, the seeker in this book learns some simple, powerful skills that are readily communicable. These skills allow him to lose weight, stop smoking, and accomplish many other goals in his life, quickly and easily.

These skills are called self-management skills, and this book will teach you how to become a self-manager.

Why the management lingo? Because the single most important person you manage is not on your staff or among your family members or friends. You may even forget sometimes that this individual needs good management. The face of this individual is usually invisible to you, and yet it is the most important face in the world. You can see this face only in a mirror — for the face is your very own.

Isn't there a contradiction here? How can you manage yourself? Isn't managing what we do to others?

The pages that follow will show you

famed behaviorist B. F. Skinner. Skinner was a brilliant scientist, but I learned as much from watching him behave as I did from his scientific work. Skinner was the happiest, most productive, most creative person I've ever known, largely because he was so skilled at self-management. We can all profit by learning more about how he lived his life. "Uncle Fred," one of the characters in this book, is modeled, just a little, after Burrhus Frederic Skinner.

I wrote this book with relative ease by using some of the techniques described in it. From time to time, I'll alert you to how I've benefitted personally from these techniques by adding a "Personal Bubble" to the page.

By the way, this book is different from most other "self-help" books for three reasons:

First, self-management techniques have been empirically tested. They work. I am not relaying folk wisdom, common sense, or my personal credo. I am conveying, in allegory form, a body of basic and applied research in the behavioral sciences.

Second, self-management is practical and straightforward. You needn't change your "attitudes" or "beliefs" or "personality" to be a good self-manager. No "willpower" is required. No mysterious psychic entities are involved. The

that we do manage ourselves and that self-management involves fundamental skills that anyone can master. A few people are already excellent self-managers; through luck and ingenuity, they have acquired appropriate skills. Most people are not so fortunate.

Good self-managers live good lives. They live up to their potential in their careers and their relationships. They keep their weight under control. They eat healthful foods. They solve problems as they arise. They feel good about themselves. They are creative in every aspect of their lives. They manage others more effectively.

Bad self-managers complain a lot. They bite their nails. They overeat. They lose keys. They procrastinate. They go to bed too late. They are daunted by simple challenges. They have frequent depressions. They give up.

You can learn to be a more skillful self-manager, no matter what your current level of expertise and no matter what challenges you face. If you're like most people, you'll be amazed at what a difference some very simple skills can make.

I've been studying self-management — both in others and, of course, in myself — for nearly twenty years. And during my doctoral training at Harvard, I worked daily for five years with one of the most skillful self-managers in the world, message is: If you want to change yourself, here is what you do. Period.

Third, self-management techniques are widely applicable. If you master the three simple skills presented in this book, you will be able to tackle virtually any kind of problem. Dieting, getting organized, becoming more creative, and coping with stress are just special cases of self-management. The special cases are easy to handle when you know the general principles.

Self-management is a constant challenge because we are always growing, and circumstances are always changing. But self-management is also fun, as you will soon discover.

I hope you enjoy the pages that follow, and I know you will profit from them.

Robert Epstein, Ph.D.
Cardiff by the Sea, California

THE

SEARCH

SELF-HELP WITHOUT THE HYPE

Once there was a young man who wasn't entirely happy with himself. He had his share of success, but his life seemed out of control in many ways.

He ate too much, and he ate foods that were unhealthful.

He procrastinated.

He had tried to stop smoking, but he could never stop for long.

He kept losing his keys. Sometimes he locked them in his car.

He didn't get enough exercise.

Sometimes he lost his temper and shouted at people he loved. He felt terrible afterwards.

He had trouble getting things done, and he always seemed to be behind.

He went to bed too late and did not sleep soundly. He hated his alarm clock.

He also bit his fingernails.

Sometimes he wasn't worried about these things. "Everyone is like me," he said to himself. "Everyone's life is in disarray. No one's perfect."

He had plenty of friends who were overweight or overtired. He knew plenty of people who procrastinated or lost things. It's natural and inevitable to be behind in one's work— he was sure of it.

But then, every now and then, out of the corner of his eye, he would spot an exception. He tried hard not to notice, but sometimes he couldn't help himself.

There were, it seemed, at least a few people who were "in control."

These exceptional people seemed happy and healthy. They were slim and well-rested. They exercised regularly. They had never smoked, or they had successfully quit smoking.
They achieved their goals.

One day the young man was studying his image in a mirror. He was disturbed by the bags under his eyes, by the sallowness of his complexion, and by what seemed to be the beginning of a double chin.

He asked himself, "Are the exceptional people really different from me, or do they just know something I don't?

"If they know something, just what do they know?

"Can I learn it?

"Who can I ask?"

The young man thought and thought.

He knew a young woman who always seemed to keep her life in order. He called her and asked, "What's your secret? How do you manage to get yourself to do what you want to do?"

The woman replied, "I don't know. I don't think about it at all. I just do it."

The young man was discouraged. Perhaps there was no secret, or perhaps it was something you couldn't put into words.

He called his parents and asked, "Did I miss some important lesson when I was growing up? Can you tell me now how I might take better care of myself than I do?"

His parents replied, "There is nothing more we can teach you. We taught you what we ourselves know. We did our very best."

He spoke with a clergyman, and he spoke with the teachers who had touched his life when he was young. "What's the secret?" he asked.

No one could tell him.

UNCLE FRED

Then the young man remembered his old Uncle Fred.

Uncle Fred wasn't really his uncle. He was really just a friend of the family.

When the young man was a child, he loved visits from Uncle Fred, as did the other children in the neighborhood. Uncle Fred told great stories that seemed to unravel as they went along, and the children were always important characters in each story. It was as if Uncle Fred were composing each story on the spot.

He invented new games for the children to play, and he always joined the children in the games. He laughed as he played, even though — curiously — he never won.

He never missed a birthday, and he always gave books for presents — fun books, usually adventure novels or mysteries. Sometimes when the pages were dog-eared coming out of the wrapping paper, Uncle Fred would say, "Oh, well, I read it first, of course! I wanted to make sure you'd like it."

Uncle Fred loved to be alive. You could see it in his face. He grinned a lot, with the mischievous grin of a kid in a candy store. Even though he was middle-aged when the young man first met him, Fred's eyes always sparkled with boyish youth and vitality.

The young man had kept in touch with Uncle Fred over the years, and the vitality never seemed to fade.

As the young man thought more about Uncle Fred, he began to see him in a new light. He had heard from his parents that Uncle Fred had had difficulties when he was young but that he had overcome them through extensive study of some sort. Fred must have learned something important when he was young, and, whatever it was he had learned, he must have learned it well. He was productive in his profession, even in old age. He was creative in every aspect of his life, and he was incredibly happy.

"Uncle Fred must surely know the secrets of good self-care, and he must be a master of them," the young man concluded.

"I'll bet he will be able to tell me what those secrets are. If anyone can tell me, it will be Uncle Fred."

Even though Fred was in his late 70s, he still worked part-time. "You've got to stay active," he always said. "He who lives by his wits dies with his wits."

The young man called him at his office number. As usual, Uncle Fred answered the phone, rather than have his secretary do so.

"It's always impressed me that you answer your own phone, Uncle Fred," said the young man.

"There's no substitute for face-to-face communication," Fred replied. "Unless, of course, you're on the telephone," he added. The young man envisioned him grinning at the other end of the line, and indeed he was.

The young man asked for an appointment, and they arranged to meet at Uncle Fred's home the following week.

THE

FIRST

SECRET:

MODIFYING
YOUR ENVIRONMENT

Uncle Fred lived in a modest home on a quiet, tree-lined street. He greeted the young man warmly at the door.

"Thanks very much for dropping by!" he exclaimed.

The young man followed him down a narrow flight of stairs to Fred's basement study. Fred sat at his desk and offered his guest a comfortable chair.

"Well," he said, "from the look in your eye, I suspect this is going to be a very serious discussion. I'd better batten down the hatches." He grinned that famous grin, reached to the back of his telephone, and detached the cord.

"There!" he exclaimed. "We're safe now!"

Then he raised the cord in front of his face and, addressing himself to the little plastic plug, said with a smile, "Now, what seems to be the problem? Is it a feeling of being disconnected?"

The young man laughed heartily. He already felt better.

After a short pause, the young man took a deep breath and began his story. He explained that he had several problems — a large set of them, actually. He spoke about his weight and his diet, his memory quirks, his lack of exercise, his short temper, his procrastinating, his sleeping difficulties, and all the other problems that concerned him.

Uncle Fred was a very patient listener, so the young man left out nothing. The older man nodded at times with a concerned look on his face, and sometimes he smiled and shook his head knowingly. He let his guest speak without interruption.

When the young man had finished listing his concerns, he explained that he now believed that there were "secrets" to taking care of oneself.

"And you must know them, Uncle Fred, because your life has always seemed so satisfying and smooth. Will you tell me how you do it?"

"Well," said Fred when his visitor finally concluded, "you do seem to have a problem. But only one.

"And, yes, I can indeed help you."

"But it will cost you," said Uncle Fred.

"Cost me?" said the young man. "I don't understand."

"I don't mean money," Fred replied. "I mean that if you want me to help you, you will have to give me your solemn promise on a few matters."

"What matters?" said the young man.

"First, you must promise to come back two more times after today. Next week and the following week will be fine. We will need these visits to complete your training.

"Second, you must promise to keep records of your progress.

"And third, if you find the training valuable, you must promise to train others when your own training has been completed."

"That's all?" asked the young man. "You will give me your secrets to good living and for so little in return?"

"That's all," said Fred. Then he grinned again. "Come to think of it, a crisp red apple would be nice at some point. It's traditional."

"Let's begin the training," said Uncle Fred. He paused and then said, dramatically, "I'm happy and productive because I'm a self-manager."

"A what?" asked the young man.

"A self-manager," Fred repeated, with characteristic patience.

"You have only one problem, not dozens. You are not a self-manager. That's your problem. Fortunately, it's not hard to correct."

"How can I become a self-manager, and why do there seem to be so few of them around?" asked the visitor.

Uncle Fred leaned back in his chair, knitted his brows, and touched the tips of his fingers together, forming an inverted V in front of his chin. As the young man soon learned, this was the posture Fred assumed when he was about to give a lengthy speech.

"You can become a self-manager by learning and then practicing a few simple skills. They're easy to learn and easy to put into practice.

"There are many self-management skills, but almost all of them fall into three categories — what you would call my three 'secrets.' Today I'll tell you the first, next week the second, and the following week the third. You can put each one into practice after our meetings."

Fred continued: "Why are there so few self-managers? That's not an easy question. I guess the simplest answer is that most people just haven't learned the skills. Even people who have some of the skills just haven't thought about them. They can't identify them, and so they have trouble teaching them to other people.

"For example, I never lock myself out of my car because I always check for my key before closing the door. I even use a little verse to help remind me: 'Got the keys? Then close it, please.' I made that up myself, you know," said Fred with a smile.

"The point is, when in your life does someone teach you a little self-management technique like that? Do parents teach such skills? Not universally, I'm afraid. Is self-management part of the school curriculum? I think not. Are self-management skills taught at religious services? Well, perhaps here more than elsewhere, but not nearly enough.

"Most people just don't know about the skills. I guess that's the first answer to your question."

PERSONAL BUBBLE

On vacation at Disney World with my children a few years ago, my older son locked the car key in our rental car. It was a Sunday morning, and it took hours to get help.

The day we returned from vacation, I taped a spare car key in my wallet. Just a few weeks later, I locked my key case in my own car. The key in the wallet saved the day.

We all stumble onto tricks like this to help us run our lives, but Uncle Fred is going to take you much further — all the way to general principles.

Good traveling!

"There's another answer, however," Fred continued. "In our society, we are often discouraged from becoming self-managers. Our heads are filled with notions that just aren't very helpful and that interfere with good self-management."

"What do you mean, Uncle Fred?" the young man asked.

"I'll tell you only if you promise not to get your back up. Just keep an open mind."

"Sure, okay. I promise," said the young man, solemnly.

"All right, then," said Fred, "let's take this 'will power' idea as an example. There are millions of people out there struggling to quit smoking or lose weight or exercise through the use of 'will power.' But what on earth is 'will power'?"

Without looking, Fred reached to his right and instantly produced a dictionary from a nearby shelf. "Let's see," he said. "The dictionary defines 'will power' as 'energetic determination,' and — just a moment — it defines 'determination' as 'firm or fixed purpose,' and — let's see — it defines 'purpose' as 'resolution or determination,' and we already know what 'determination' means. It means 'purpose.' So 'purpose' means 'determination,' and 'determination' means 'purpose.'"

Uncle Fred continued to flip pages, looking quite determined as he did so. This, it seems, was one of the ways he had fun in his old age.

He continued, "Hmmm. It defines 'resolution' as 'the quality of being resolute; firmness or determination,' and we already know what 'determination' means, don't we? It means 'purpose,' which brings us back to 'determination' and 'resolution' again.

"So now we just need to check the word 'resolute,' and everything should fall into place. Here it is. 'Resolute — firmly determined in purpose.' Well, that solves it, don't you think? 'Will power' means 'determination.' And what does 'determination' mean? 'Purpose.' And what does 'purpose' mean? 'Determination.' Or 'resolution.' And what does 'resolution' mean? 'Purpose'! We go around and around, you see, and never really find out much at all.

"You need to beware of dictionaries. They really don't contain the meanings of words; they just contain other words.

"The real problem, though, is not the vagueness of the concept of 'will power.' The problem is that when someone advises you to use 'will power,' they're not specifying any behavior. They're not telling you what, precisely, to do.

"They're telling you to be 'determined' — but now what? What should you actually do?"

The young man felt frustrated. He had always believed in 'will power.' But now — perhaps momentarily swayed by Uncle Fred's spell — he began to wonder about it. What is will power, anyway? And what on earth was Fred proposing as an alternative?

"I'm not sure I buy everything you're saying, Uncle Fred," said the man. "But I admit that will power has never seemed to work for me. I've tried and tried to change, but without success. Trying isn't enough. I guess that's what you're telling me. But what else is there?"

"A great deal, my boy. A great deal. You don't need to be Rambo or Superman to change yourself. Selfchange is easy and painless when you know the three secrets. Let's try the first one, shall we? I think you're ready now."

"The first secret of self-management — or, to be more precise, the first skill — is the easiest, the most flexible, and the most powerful."

Again without looking, Fred reached out to a cubbyhole above his desk and produced a piece of white paper. He reached out again and produced a marker. Then he drew a large M in the upper left-hand corner of the sheet:

M

"Remember this **M**," he said. "It stands for *Modify Your Environment*." He proceeded to write those words on the sheet next to the **M**, like this:

MODIFY YOUR ENVIRONMENT

"The simplest way to change yourself is to change your world," said Uncle Fred. "I can't overstate the importance of this. You gain tremendous power over yourself when you master this simple technique."

"I don't understand," said the young man. "If I change the space around me in some way — and I'm really not sure I understand what you mean by that — I'm still not any different."

"*Au contraire*," said Uncle Fred. "If you make the right changes, you are very different afterwards. Let me explain, and let me explain further what I mean by *Modify Your Environment*."

"If you want to know who someone is — or even who you are — you need to look at behavior — what someone does and says and thinks. That's what I mean by behavior. We say people change when we see their behavior change. In a very real sense, we are our behavior.

"If a man attends church, speaks of a love of God, and behaves morally, you may consider him upright and religious. If he stops attending church, says he has lost his faith, and behaves immorally, you will judge him less favorably, and you will say he has changed. What we do and say and think is who we are.

"If you want to change yourself, you need simply to change the way you behave, and the simplest way to do that is to change your world in some way. When your behavior has changed, you will feel differently about yourself You will feel that you have changed."

The young man was skeptical. "It can't be that easy. That's impossible. A secret like that would be worth, well, millions!"

Uncle Fred shook his head and smiled. "I doubt that the idea is worth much money, but it's true. Changing your immediate environment is the simplest, most powerful way to change yourself. Perhaps some examples would help make this clearer."

"You know me as a writer, do you not?" said Uncle Fred. The young man nodded. "And you know me as a man who loves to write, isn't that so?" The pupil nodded again.

"Good, good. And you are correct. I do love to write. It's an absolute joy for me. And it comes almost effortlessly. But you see, I created that me — that person who loves to write — the person who sits here before you. And I did this in large part by modifying my environment."

"That's pretty hard to believe," said the visitor.

"But it's true!" said Uncle Fred. "I used to hate to write, but I yearned so much to write more and to enjoy what I was doing. I asked myself, 'How might I change the space around me to accomplish my writing goals?' Over time, I found many, many ways to do that."

"What did you do?" the young man queried.

"Take a look around you," said Fred, "and tell me what you see."

The visitor glanced around quickly. He saw nothing very unusual at first, nothing that seemed to explain the kind of radical personality change Uncle Fred had described.

Then he realized that what seemed to be a sofa on the other side of the study might be a bed in disguise. A crazy thought went through his head.

"Uncle Fred, did you put your bed in your study so that you would write more?"

"Bravo, my student!" exclaimed Fred. "Good detective work! I brought my bed downstairs nearly twenty years ago for precisely the reason you gave. Now, when I lie in bed and the urge to write strikes — pow! — I jump out of bed and go to it! When my bed was upstairs, I never did that. I wanted to, but my study seemed too far away. For a while, I made the mistake of labeling myself 'lazy.' But I wasn't 'lazy,' really. My bed was just too far from my study."

"That's amazing, Uncle Fred, but I also must admit that it sounds a bit eccentric. I mean, couldn't you have brought your desk upstairs, rather than bringing your bed downstairs? Wouldn't most people have done it the latter way?"

"Another very perceptive comment," replied Fred. "First of all, most people wouldn't have moved anything anywhere; they would have relied on 'will power' and told themselves they were lazy because they weren't achieving their goals. They would have suffered a great deal and eventually quit writing. What a great waste!

"I tried bringing the desk upstairs, but that didn't work at all. Far too many distractions up there. Windows, televisions, clothes to wash, and that darned refrigerator. I spent more time eating than writing. The space upstairs occasioned too many behaviors that competed with serious writing.

"Am I eccentric for bringing the bed down here? You bet! That's the beauty of self-management. It's entirely private and personal, and it's also different for every individual. You will need to find what works for you. Bringing the bed down here worked well for me."

PERSONAL BUBBLE

My own study is unsuited for writing, in part, because it contains three telephones. Mark Twain approached the problem by having his phone installed in an out-of-the-way closet, but these are different times.

To write this book, I changed my environment radically. I spent half of each week living like a hermit in New Hampshire.

It's the ultimate environment change: *Get out of town.*

"Is that all you see around us?" continued Fred. "Just the bed?"

The young man looked around again. "Well, that looks like a tape recorder on the small table by your bed. Is that right?"

"Very good," said Uncle Fred. "That tape recorder helps keep mywork creative. When a good idea strikes me in the middle of the night, I reach over and press the record button, and I capture my idea on tape before it disappears. Perhaps we'll talk more about creativity after we've covered more of the basics."

"You mean you can use self-management skills to make yourself more creative? That's unbelievable! This is worth billions!" said the young man.

"That's quite a fixation you have on money," said Uncle Fred. "I'll take fifty percent of anything you make on this." Fred laughed.

"To answer your question: Yes, you can enhance your creativity greatly through self-management. For now, let's focus on my writing. Look at my desk. Do you see the shelves and cubbyholes all around it? Gradually over the years, I've arranged them in a very special way. They contain the tools I need to write, and they're all immediately at hand — my thesaurus and dictionaries, my collections of quotations, my guides to good writing, my typewriter, paper, pencils, pens, erasers, and so on. I can get to anything I need quickly and easily, without even thinking. By having everything at hand, I make my work smooth and pleasant, and I eliminate silly excuses for not working."

"I noticed," said the young man, "that you didn't seem to look when you grabbed that dictionary earlier. It just appeared."

Uncle Fred shut his eyes tightly. "Want to know when Abraham Lincoln was born?" He reached out to his right and *Webster's Biographical Dictionary* materialized instantly. He handed it to his incredulous guest.

"1809, Uncle Fred."

Fred opened his eyes. "Very good, son.
I think you're getting the idea."

"Do you ever get fidgety?" asked Uncle Fred.

"Sure," said the visitor. "When I go to a ballet or a symphony, I squirm in my seat. I can't wait for intermission. Sometimes it happens at my office too. It can be torture."

"Look at my seat," Fred said. Uncle Fred was sitting on a padded office chair. It seemed fairly standard, except for a tear on the side of the seat cushion. Some yellow foam protruded from the tear.

"It looks fairly — ragged," said the young man, awkwardly.

"Ragged, yes, but very, very comfortable," said Fred. "You see, I had been fidgeting. While working at my desk, I'd start to squirm. I'd have to get up and pace or take a walk. Then I thought, what's going on here? Could it be some aspect of my environment? Could it be the chair itself?

"I slit open the sides of the cushion, removed some foam here and there, and stuffed in some new foam. I shaped the cushion until it fit my behind perfectly. And it worked!"

Fred's face gleamed with excitement. "I worked much longer, and the fidgeting all but disappeared. I realize that altering a seat cushion sounds a little odd, but I got more work done as a result. We're talking bottom line here!"

Fred grinned ear to ear, and the young man, in spite of himself, laughed and laughed.

"Shall we take a break now?" asked Uncle Fred.

"Sure, but I don't need one," replied the visitor. Then, suddenly embarrassed, he exclaimed, "Oh, you must be tired! I forget about your age because you act so young!"

"I'm not tired," said Fred. "But I found long ago that I think better if I take frequent breaks. I put a sign on the wall to help remind me." He motioned to a framed picture on the wall near his desk. "Look there," he said.

In the frame was the following in large letters: "Hour Power."

"Hour Power," Fred explained, "is short for 'Break on the hour for more THINKING POWER.'"

"Wow, that's great, Uncle Fred! You discovered something about yourself and then modified your environment to help remind you! And what a great practice. I'm all for breaks."

They walked up the narrow stairs to the kitchen on the first floor, and the young man helped Fred prepare some tea and butter cookies. They relaxed and talked about the news and family matters as they sipped their tea. The young man started to ask about self-management, and Fred held out his hand and said, "Hold it. This is a break. Just relax now. There's plenty of time for serious talk after our tea. Remember the sign?"

The young man and his ersatz uncle recited together: "Hour Power!"

"Wow," said the young man.

And he relaxed.

HOUR POWER

After their tea, they returned to the study, and Fred continued the lesson: "You can modify your environment in many different ways, with many different effects. And you can change almost any of your behaviors with this technique alone.

"Come, let's take a short walk." Fred led his guest into a room adjacent to the study. They approached a standard exercise bike.

"Years ago," said Fred, "I didn't exercise regularly. I even had some heart problems, and my physician urged me to exercise more. I took her advice seriously, but I wasn't consistent. I'd exercise for a few weeks, then stop for a while, feel guilty, and start again.

"Finally, I faced the fact that I needed some management — some self-management, of course.

"I asked, can I change my space in some way to tackle the problem? I wanted to exercise every morning, without exception. Was there something that I already did every morning? Could I tie exercising to that activity?

"Then it hit me: Every morning I watched the news. Every morning. I'm a regular news hound, you know. So the solution was simple: As you can see, I mounted a small television set over the handle bars. Except when I've been sick or traveling, I've exercised every morning since. And now that I do both activities at once, I enjoy each one more."

PERSONAL BUBBLE

I'm not much of a television fan, so Uncle Fred's technique wouldn't be right for me. But I love to read. I made my own exercise bike more appealing by attaching a book holder to the wall next to the bike. I also added a small reading lamp to the book holder and an electric fan to blow a steady stream of air in my face as I pedaled and read. It took a week or two of adjustments before the arrangement was truly comfortable for me. Once it was, exercising became a real joy.

"Many, many different types of problems — sleep problems, work problems,
procrastination, diet problems — every
problem you mentioned today, and many
others beside can be handled by modifying
your environment. Come," said Uncle Fred,
"let me show you something else."

Fred led the way back to the stair-
case. The young man said, "We're going up
again? I didn't know selfmanagement was
going to be such work!"

Fred chuckled. "I keep important
things on separate floors deliberately. I get
a lot more exercise that way. I place some
things close together — as you saw at my
desk — and other things far apart. In each
case I'm interested in affecting my behavior
in some way. I put writing implements
close together to make writing pleasurable
and smooth. I put other things far apart to
get more exercise or to keep things out of
sight.

"Remember," said Fred as he mounted the stairs, "'distance yourself!' Place
things close together or far apart to get the
behavior you want from yourself."

"Distance yourself!" the young man
repeated. "What a wonderfully simple idea
that is."

"Simple, powerful, and underutilized,"
said Fred.

PERSONAL BUBBLE

When, in my 30s, I became concerned about weight gain, I applied the "distance" rule very literally. When I went shopping, I began to park fairly far from the entrance to the store. This meant extra exercise and calorie savings nearly every day, and it also meant that I was spared the frustration of searching for that perfect parking spot — you know, the one that's just inches away from where you're going?

I guess I distanced myself from calories.

At the landing at the top of the stairs, Fred paused and turned to his guest. He reached out and placed his hand on the young man's arm.

"I'm not so young anymore, you know."

The young man was startled. He didn't know what to say, so he said nothing.

"Many of the problems I deal with in my life are very different than the problems you described. Old people have special needs and special problems. Self-management is especially useful when you get old. Let me show you my reading chair, and you'll see what I mean."

They approached a recliner chair in the living room. A tall lamp-like object stood beside the chair.

"This device," said Fred, pointing to the tall object, "is not a conventional lamp. You see, my vision has deteriorated over the years. At some point I found that reading had become unpleasant. I was reading less and less, and new glasses didn't make much difference. So what did I ask myself?" Fred tilted his index finger toward his visitor.

"You asked yourself how you might modify your environment to help, right?"

"Right!" said Fred. "Eventually, I ordered this gizmo from a catalog. It's an illuminated magnifying glass. Here, sit down and try it."

The young man sat, and Fred handed him a magazine. An arm on the special lamp supported a flat glass disk about six inches in diameter. Fred swung the disk over the magazine and switched on a light that was attached to the disk.

"Wow," said the young man, "what incredible magnification! The fine print looks huge and very bright."

"I have a smaller version in my pocket," said Fred, producing what looked like a flashlight with a magnifying glass at the end.

"The point is to construct your world so that it makes you the kind of person you want to be. Gizmos can help."

As if to emphasize the point, a buzzer immediately sounded on Uncle Fred's wristwatch.

"Time for my afternoon vitamins," said Fred. He walked into the kitchen, his visitor trailing behind, and brought a plastic box down from a shelf. He swung open the lid. Inside were several dozen small compartments, some of which held pills of various colors. On the inside of the lid was a white piece of paper with boxes drawn on it corresponding to the small compartments.

"The pill holder is a great invention," Fred said. "I load it up at the beginning of the week, and on the lid I write the times and days and types of pills. The timer and box guarantee that I will take the right pill at the right time. Without them, I used to make mistakes. We old people can be pretty forgetful, you know."

"It's not just old people, Uncle Fred. You wouldn't believe how forgetful I can be!"

Fred swallowed a pill.

"Timers, too," he said, pointing to his watch, "are part of our environment. When you set an alarm clock at night, you're modifying your environment so that it will wake you up the next morning at a certain time. Setting an alarm clock before bedtime is about the only self-management skill that is universally taught in our culture. Unfortunately, the general practice of modifying the environment is never taught — only this one case. What a shame!"

The young man looked uneasy. "Uh, would you mind if I took a break outside for a few minutes?" he said.

"Cigarettes," said Fred. "Sure, of course. I used to smoke too — a long time ago. Did you know that?"

"I can hardly believe it. I can't believe you ever did anything so harmful," said the young man.

"Oh, I had my moments," chuckled Fred. "And keep in mind that when I was young, we didn't know cigarettes were so bad. The famous Surgeon General's report didn't appear until the 1960s, you know. But I beat smoking — and I'm not going to tell you how I did so. You'll understand why a week from now, I suspect. Now go take your break. You know where I'll be."

The young man, puzzled and somewhat frustrated by Fred's unwillingness to say how he quit smoking, went outside.

"I think you're ready now to return home and try your first self-management project," said Fred when his guest returned.

"But Uncle Fred," said the young man, "you've only told me how you've solved some of your problems. You haven't told me how to solve any of mine."

Fred smiled and his eyes twinkled. His hands came together in the inverted V. Another speech was coming.

"I need to tell you a fish tale," said Fred. "It's actually just a short lesson from an ancient commentary on the Bible. It goes like this: 'Give a man a fish, and he will not be hungry. Teach a man to fish, and he will never be hungry.'

"You want me to give you a fish — to advise you on how to solve some of your problems. But today I have taken a step toward teaching you to fish. I have provided you with a simple skill that will help you solve your own problems. This is far more valuable than a fish.

"I never gave you any specific advice today about any of your problems. Instead, I told you about a simple and powerful technique — modifying your environment — and then I gave you examples of how I used this technique to manage my own behavior. This was deliberate on my part, and you must do the same when you train others. Don't hand out fish if you can help it! People hand out fish all the time. People just love to give advice. But hardly anyone knows how to fish. I am teaching you how to fish.

"Let me put it another way. Self-managers think for themselves. Confidence is skill. Self-managers are confident about their ability to tackle problems because they have the skills they need to do so.

"Do you know about 'mutual dependency'?" Fred asked.

The young man shook his head.

"It's a messy situation, all too common in marriages," said Fred. "Each spouse thinks the other one is supposed to do something — wash the dishes, for example — so neither one does it, and each feels hurt and angry over the other person's faiure. The dishes can get piled rather-high."

"Sure, I know about that," said the young man. "My brother and I used to have that problem. We each thought the other was supposed to vacuum the rug. So neither of us did it. It made our mom very angry."

"Exactly," said Fred. "People who haven't yet learned the secrets of self-management often have a similar problem. They are dependent. They can't depend on themselves for answers, so they constantly seek help from others — therapists, weight-loss products, clinics, and so forth — or they go without and live with their life's dishes piled high.

"Self-managers, on the other hand, have the skills to solve their own problems. They are self-reliant. They don't blame other people or mysterious forces for their problems. They work hard, and keep working hard, to solve them.

"So now you must go off into the world — on your own, but with new knowledge — and think for yourself. When we began our discussion, you promised to keep records of your progress and to return next week. Here, specifically, is what I'd like you to do."

Fred wrote down the assignment as he explained it to his guest:

SELF-MANAGEMENT
Week #1 Assignment

1.
2. *Select a behavior to change.*
3. *Keep a record of when it occurs.*
   Modify your environment to help
   produce the change you desire.
   Come back again next week for the
   second secret!
   Best of luck!

   Uncle Fred

"I'd also like you to call Susan, a young woman who came to me years ago with some very serious dilemmas. I turned her into a self-manager, of course. See what she has to say about all this. I think you'll find your visit well worthwhile. It will give you another perspective." Fred wrote down a phone number and handed it to his guest.

"I should warn you that Susan will not be what you expect," Fred continued, "because you probably expect her to be something like me. But it's very important that you meet with her. She can teach you something about self-management much better than I can. And the lesson she can teach you is essential to good self-management. Be sure to meet with her, and — well, keep your eyes open."

Another mystery, thought the young man. "I'll call Susan," he said, "and I'll try to follow through on the assignment you've given me, but I'm not very optimistic. You've made the whole thing sound too easy, too pat. I guess I'm still a bit skeptical about the whole thing. It sounds great, but I doubt that it will work for me. And it just can't be as easy as you say."

"Quite understandable skepticism, my young friend. Quite understandable. But self-management is easy, as you will see. I haven't exaggerated one single jot."

Fred picked up the severed telephone line and said to it, "Well, well. I guess your problems are all solved, yes? You may go home now."

He reattached the cord and sent his visitor home.

THE

FIRST

WEEK:

KICKING
AN OLD HABIT

The young man felt very different after his encounter with Uncle Fred. In spite of his skepticism, he felt exhilarated. He felt that change was possible — at least for Uncle Fred. And, after all, Fred had given him exactly what he asked for: The young man had come to Fred believing that self-change involved skill and knowledge. Uncle Fred had reinforced his suspicions and had shared some of his knowledge.

But would it work?

The young man's first task was to choose a behavior to change. He was dismayed at first. There were too many to choose from.

He settled on nail-biting. It was a small problem but one that had nagged him most of his life. He felt that if he could beat this one, he would gain the confidence he needed to take on more serious problems. And if he were successful, he would see the results. "They will be right at hand," he said to himself, grinning as Uncle Fred might have.

It seemed like a good place to start.

His second task was to keep records of the behavior. But how should he keep records of his nail biting? Uncle Fred hadn't said. And Uncle Fred withheld such information deliberately, didn't he?

A newspaper lay on his lap as he contemplated the matter. Suddenly, he realized he was biting at a fingernail. He said to himself, I should record this, but I have no pencil and paper handy. He looked down at the paper and thought, why not just tear a little notch in the edge of the paper when I catch myself nail-biting? He reached down and made a small tear.

That's one, he thought.

He soon realized that he could improve this system easily. He tore off seven pieces of paper from a small pad and wrote abbreviations for each weekday on each of the pieces, along with the dates. He wrote "nail-biting" on the first sheet and drew a rough time scale along the edge. Then he stapled the sheets together. He put his makeshift record book in his pocket.

Now, when I catch myself nail-biting, he thought, I'll make a little tear on the correct sheet for the day and at the right spot for the time. When something significant is happening that seems related to nail-biting, I'll jot it down on the paper! No sweat.

<u>NAIL-BITING</u>

3 –

6 –

9 –

NOON –

3 –

6 –

9 –

MIDNIGHT –

MONDAY, OCTOBER 21

That takes care of items 1 and 2, he thought, but how can I modify my environment to change nail-biting? This is crazy.

He thought about the problem off and on during the day, making small tears in his record book when he caught himself biting his nails. He was tempted to call Uncle Fred for advice, but he knew what Fred would say: "It's fishing we're after, not fish. Think for yourself!"

He was even tempted to quit altogether. But then he'd have to face Uncle Fred, and he didn't want to let the old man down. He'd promised to visit Fred next week, so he'd just have to stay with the program for the moment.

Fortunately, he noticed two things at the end of the first full day: First, he didn't appear to be biting his nails very much — less than usual, it seemed. What was happening? And second, he usually bit hangnails and rough edges exclusively, as if he were trying to smooth things out. He had never noticed that before. Hmmm.

He implemented a simple plan — so simple that he was sure it would fail. But isn't setting an alarm clock simple? And wasn't the television set in front of Uncle Fred's exercise bike simple?

He went to his local pharmacy and bought fifty nail files and ten nail clippers, and then he spread them around. He planted them everywhere:his pants pockets, his coat pockets, his bathroom, his kitchen, his recliner chair, his office desk — everywhere he bit his nails.

He was astonished at the result: He began grooming his nails instead of biting them, and he wasn't even trying! Everywhere he looked, there were nail files and clippers, so he used them to smooth his nails. And smooth nails just weren't any fun to bite.

After just a few days, his record book showed no more tears.

He felt just a little giddy.

How far could this stuff go? Had he actually solved his nail-biting problem with a small expenditure and a few nail files?

Should he start on a second behavior?

Perhaps Susan could shed some light.

SUSAN,

A REMARKABLE

TEACHER

Susan, it turned out, was a school teacher. She asked the young man to meet her in the staff lounge of her school during the lunch hour.

She greeted him warmly as he entered the lounge.

"Hi!" she said, reaching out to take his right hand in both of hers. "You must be Fred's friend."

"Yes, and I guess you're Susan, right?"

"You've got it! Let's sit and talk for a few minutes, shall we?"

"Sure," said the young man, "and thanks for letting me see you today."

She led him to an easy chair and sat facing him. He sized her up quickly and was a bit surprised by what he saw. Susan was in her late twenties and had a kind and intelligent look about her, but she was far from flawless. She was a bit over-weight, for one thing, and her hair was disheveled. An unruly wisp of brown hair had fallen in front of her left eye.

Somehow, the young man had thought she would be perfect, like Uncle Fred seemed to be, but her rough edges were showing. He asked himself, "Is she really a self-manager? What important lesson could I possibly learn from her?"

"It's so great to meet another friend of Fred's," Susan said pleasantly. She moved the lock of hair away from her eye. "And he tells me that he's known you since you were born. It must have been great to know him while you were growing up."

"Yes," said the young man, "it was great. Uncle Fred was like Santa Claus year-round. Every child on the block would come over during his visits. How did you meet him?"

"Oh, my dad was involved in a business venture with him years ago," Susan replied. "When I started having personal problems, my dad suggested I talk to him, and he was a great help. No, he was more than that. He may have saved my life."

"You're kidding!" exclaimed the young man. "Are you claiming that self-management saved your life? I know it's supposed to be good, but that sounds a bit much."

"I guess I'm exaggerating," Susan replied, "but it's just because I'm so grateful to Fred for helping me. You see —"

Susan paused, looked around, and then lowered her voice.

"I was falling apart . . . . My marriage had failed and I was taking care of my son on my own. I wasn't earning enough money, and I was completely stressed out at work. I was very overweight, smoking heavily, showing up late for everything, and not getting enough sleep. I got sick — minor problems at first, but then I got stomach problems and one infection after another. My immune system was deteriorating, I think."

She paused again, looking a bit embarrassed. "I hope I'm not making you uncomfortable by telling you all this," she said. "I guess it's because we have the same teacher . . . I just feel I can trust you."

"No problem," said the young man. "I mean, you must realize that I've been having problems too, or I wouldn't be here now. You can tell me anything at all."

He felt a little surprised that he said this. He wasn't used to being so open, and he certainly had never been comfortable listening to other people's problems. He was usually too concerned about his own. Had a single visit with Uncle Fred changed him in some way? Could it be that he was feeling more confident?

"What have you been going through?" Susan asked.

Again, to his surprise, he found himself telling Susan — a complete stranger — about the difficulties that had brought him to Fred. She listened raptly, and perhaps for that reason, he continued to feel at ease. He even told her how skeptical he had felt about self-management.

"You're a great listener," he finally told her.

"Thanks," she said brightly.

"How did you manage to solve all your problems?" he asked. "Was it really self-management?"

Susan hesitated. "Well," she said, "I never really did solve all my problems." She blushed and lowered her head a bit, as if to call attention to her weight. The lock of hair fell into her face again. "But I used the techniques to quit smoking, to get myself to work on time, to change my diet — just about everything — nearly a complete overhaul in six months. And my medical problems disappeared! I guess my lifestyle just hadn't been very healthful. I'm doing much better now, and I feel good about the future."

"That's pretty remarkable," said the young man. "I can see why you like Uncle Fred so much."

Abruptly, Susan changed the subject.

"I also used to say the words 'you know' a lot," she said.

"Pardon me?" asked the young man.

Susan suddenly became very animated. "Well, we've talked enough about serious stuff," she said. "Would you like to hear about a great self-management program I came up with?"

"Sure," said the young man.

"I used to say 'you know' all the time," she explained. "Almost everyone says it occasionally, but I used to say it far too much. I'd say things like, 'The principal has been going out with the art teacher, you know.' Or, 'I've really got to lose some weight, you know?'" Susan smiled and her face reddened. "I solved the problem in a fairly dramatic way. Some of the other teachers here still talk about it. Can you guess what I did?"

"Well, no, I can't really —"

But Susan cut him off. "I wrote 'YOU KNOW' on a piece of paper and then attached the paper to a button on my blouse. I made sure to wear clothing with buttons during my program. Everyone could see the piece of paper and the words 'YOU KNOW.' Whenever I caught myself saying the words, I made a little tear in an edge of the paper."

The young man's face brightened. "Really?" he interjected. "I just used tearing for my nail — "

But Susan, in her enthusiasm, interrupted him again. "Oh, yes," she said. "As my Uncle Mort always says, 'Great minds think alike, and fools seldom differ.' The tearing method works great, don't you think? The point is, everyone could see the paper, the words, and the little tears. People were staring at me, and they kept asking me why I was wearing this piece of paper. They made me self-conscious. It was wonderful!

"I said 'you know' more than twenty times that first morning and only three times in the afternoon. By the end of the second day, the phrase was entirely gone. It was like a miracle. Except it wasn't, really. It was just good self-management, and it was very, very easy.

"I wore the paper a few extra days, just to be sure."

The young man said nothing, mainly because he was afraid of being interrupted again. His first impression had been confirmed. Susan was far from perfect. "And she's a self-manager?" he thought. "What's going on here? Self-managers should be like Uncle Fred!"

"Come," said Susan, "let me show you what we're doing with the children."

She led the visitor to an empty class-room filled with long tables. Hundreds of items were scattered around the tables — many traditional school items, such as workbooks, rulers, and erasers, and many unusual items, such as colored blocks, cups, strings, balls, cardboard structures, and strangely shaped objects made of col-ored clay.

"This looks like art class," said the young man.

"No," said Susan, "this is the regular classroom. But last year we incorporated self-management training into the regular curriculum. We spend just a few minutes each day teaching the children self-man-agement skills. They study more and do much better on their homework that way. And, of course, by training them early, we're preparing them for later success in school and life in general.

"At the moment, we're showing them how to enhance their creativity just by shifting things around on their desks."

The sounds of running feet came from the hallway.

"Uh, oh. They're coming back from lunch. You may as well ask the children about it yourself."

The room filled up quickly as the children scrambled to sit at the tables. Most began writing in workbooks as soon as they sat. Susan quieted the others down quickly, and they also began working.

The visitor approached a young boy in front of him. "Hi," he said. "What are you working on?"

"This is a free writing period," the boy replied. "I'm writing a story about space creatures."

"What are these for?" asked the visitor, pointing to curiously shaped clay objects in front of the boy.

"Oh, I use the clay to help me think of really strange creatures. See, I bang them or roll them or push different pieces together. Then I really think of weird stuff. When I hang upside down, that really helps too, but they don't let me do that here."

The visitor turned to a girl whose desk was walled in by large pieces of cardboard. "What is all the cardboard for?" he asked.

She stretched her hand over the wall. "Those guys," she said, pointing at, but not looking at, some children at a nearby table, "used to keep distracting me. I could have moved to a different table, but then some other people would probably have distracted me. So I just built this fence so no one would distract me."

"Doesn't your teacher mind?"

"My teacher? No, she said I was a great self-manager. She's really great, don't you think? Because she teaches us how to take care of ourselves."

At another desk he saw a girl putting a note into a large white box labeled "MY IDEA BOX."

"What's that?" he asked the girl.

"That's the box where I capture all my neat ideas," she replied. "Ideas are like rabbits. They run by really fast, and sometimes you can only see their tails or their ears. You've got to move really fast to capture them. You've got to write them down right away and then put them somewhere safe. Then you can go back to them anytime you want and do things with them."

The young man was truly amazed. He had that giddy feeling again.

"What idea did you just put in the box?" he asked.

"I was looking up at the sun, and I thought of some beautiful words, and I thought I could make them into a poem later."

She showed him the piece of paper. On it was written the following:

You warm me with your bright eye.

I want so much to see the rest of you.

May I?

Susan approached and put her hand on the girl's shoulder. "She'll be a great poet someday, don't you think? She's developing all the best tools."

The young man's opinion of Susan had been growing rapidly. He gazed at her and said, "What you're giving these children is just extraordinary. What a precious, precious gift."

"Thanks," said Susan, "but I can't take much credit. For one thing, self-management skills are pretty easy to learn, as I guess you're discovering from Uncle Fred. And children learn them especially quickly because they don't have as much to unlearn as adults do.

"Let's talk for a minute in the hall," Susan said.

She led the way out the door, turned to the young man, and then paused a moment. She brushed the hair out of her face again.

"I just wanted you to know before you left," she said, "that I'm aware of the fact that I get excited sometimes and talk a lot. I guess I can even be a bit brash at times." She hesitated again and glanced down toward the floor. "I also cut people off when I really get going. I cut you off twice when we were talking in the lounge, but I really didn't mean to. I'm sorry and I hope you'll accept my apology. I'm working on the problem — with a self-management program, of course."

The young man was staring at her. "Of course, I accept your apology," he said slowly, "and I, too, must apologize. I really misjudged you when I first met you. You're really quite — special," he said.

"Thanks," Susan replied.

"By the way," said the young man, "Uncle Fred has only told me the first secret. What are the other two?"

Susan smiled broadly, and her eyes sparkled — just like Uncle Fred's. "Sorry," she said, "but you'll have to wait for Fred to tell you. I have my own pupils," she said and turned back to her classroom.

THE

SECOND

SECRET:

MONITORING
YOUR BEHAVIOR

"Uncle Fred, I can hardly believe it, but I did it. I modified my environment in a very simple way, and my behavior changed as a result. I ended up kicking an annoying habit I've had most of my life." He held up his hands. "Look! I quit biting my nails!"

Uncle Fred, sitting comfortably in his tattered chair, smiled. "I can see the results," he said. "A very impressive start. Did you keep records, as I asked?"

The young man said proudly, "Yes, of course, and even there I made a break-through. At first I made a few tears in the edge of a newspaper, and then I came up with this simple record book that I carried in my pocket."

He handed the little book to Uncle Fred, who examined it carefully.

"Yes, yes, I see," said Fred, thought-fully. "About twenty incidents the first day, eight the second, only two on the fourth. Very nice, indeed. What is your secret?"

"My secret?" said the visitor. "My secret is your secret. I just modified my environment. I surrounded myself with nail files and clippers, and I found myself grooming my nails instead of biting them. It was like a miracle."

"And how do you feel?" asked Fred, the beginning of his famous grin playing on his lips.

"I feel great!" said the young man. "I feel like a new person! I feel like I can tackle other problems now — in fact, I was very tempted to do so before I came back here. I feel like I can change."

"Hmmm. I thought so," said Fred.

"What do you mean?"

"You are your behavior — just as I told you last week." Fred was grinning broadly now. "You made a simple change in your world, your behavior changed as a result, and you feel like a different person. You are your behavior. Do you see?"

"Yes, now I see!" said the young man. "Why this is worth —"

"— trillions?" said Fred. "Yes. I suppose it is."

"Before I reveal the second secret," said Uncle Fred, "I'd like to say a bit more about the first one. Would you mind?"

"Not at all," replied the young man, "not at all. I feel that I'm in good hands."

"Thanks," said Uncle Fred. He leaned back, and his hands formed the familiar inverted V.

"There's more to your environment than meets the eye," he began. "For one thing, your body is part of your world. One of the best ways to change your behavior is to change your body or to change bodily states."

"I don't understand, Uncle Fred. That sounds a bit like 'will power' to me."

"It's nothing like 'will power,'" Fred replied. "Here, let's try a little exercise. Close your eyes. Good. Now take a deep breath, and let it out slowly — very, very slowly."

The young man did so.

"Good," said Fred. "Now do it again . . . And again . . . And again . . . And once more . . . Good. Now — how do you feel?"

"I feel good," sighed the young man. "Very — relaxed."

"Exactly," said Fred. "You took a few deep breaths, and you feel different, relaxed. You've slowed down your pulse and added some oxygen to your blood. You engaged in some simple behavior to change your body, and you are different as a result.

"If someone insulted you now, could you handle it?"

"Well, I suppose that I could handle it better now than I might have a few minutes ago, before I took the deep breaths. Are you saying that I can change my body whenever I like and that when I do so my behavior will change?"

"Yes, quite," said Fred. "Your body is part of your environment, and you can change your body deliberately to achieve your goals, just as you can change other aspects of your environment. Deep breathing is a wonderful and very simple technique. But don't underestimate its power: Women in labor use breathing exercises to cope with tremendous pain without the aid of medication. Runners and swimmers know how important it is to breathe in certain ways before, during, and after strenuous exercise. And, nowadays, some patients are taught breathing exercises as part of treatment for handling stress, for asthma, and even for certain respiratory and cardiovascular problems.

"Remember, your body is part of your environment, and you can do many things to change your body to achieve your goals. Meditation changes your nervous system in subtle ways, with great benefits for many people. Thinking about pleasant sights and sounds can keep you calm; some therapists specialize in training people to become highly skilled in such techniques. Tightening and relaxing all of the muscle groups in your body in a progressive fashion can put you on cloud nine. Tapes are available that guide you through such exercises.

"On the other side of the coin, fifty laps in a pool or a half hour on an exercise bike will energize you — make you ready to work hard and jump high.

"What you put into your body can also affect your behavior. I used to eat pastry every morning for breakfast, but I was bothered by some dizziness later each morning, and my thinking was affected. I tried cutting out the sweets, and the problem disappeared. Eating a very large meal makes you sleepy. You tend to nap, like a lion after a kill.

"These are examples of simple things you can do to change your body, a very important part of your environment. When you're looking for ways to modify your environment, don't forget that your body is part of it.

"When you change your body," Fred continued, "you will feel different, and you will behave differently. You may cope with stress better. You may think more clearly. You may be more patient with people.

"And I'm not talking about 'will power,' said Fred, emphatically. "I'm talking about a special case of modifying your environment. I'm talking about some simple skills. Whatever you do, don't get these things confused!

"I'm up for a break," said Uncle Fred. "Will you join me?"

After a pleasant tea upstairs, Uncle Fred and his visitor returned to the basement study, and Fred said, "I haven't forgotten about the second secret, but before we discuss it, I'd be curious to hear about your visit with Susan."

The young man paused. "Well, Uncle Fred, I was amazed by the innovative work she's doing with her students, and I guess I liked her, but she sure didn't seem like a self-manager. She seemed to have a lot of faults. And she wouldn't let me talk!"

"Yes," said Fred, "she sure can go on at times. But so can I, in case you haven't noticed. We had quite a competition going during her training." Fred chuckled.

"Susan has come a long, long way," said Fred. "Her life was a shambles before she discovered self-management. She had lost her husband and her health, and she could barely care for her child. Now she faces every challenge optimistically, and she knocks them down just as fast as life serves them up.

"There's an important lesson in this, and that's why I sent you to Susan. Self-managers aren't perfect, but they are their very best. I'll never be Shakespeare or Redford, but I'll be a darned good me. And I am too!"

"I think we're ready now for the second secret," said Fred, "but I need to admit that I've not been entirely honest with you."

"You lied about something?" asked the young man.

"No, not really. It's just that I've already introduced you to the second secret — but without telling you."

"What is it?"

Fred produced the sheet of paper on which he had drawn the large M the week before. He added another large M, as follows:

MODIFY YOUR ENVIRONMENT

M

"The second secret of self-management is to *Monitor Your Behavior.*" He added these words to the second **M**:

MODIFY YOUR ENVIRONMENT

MONITOR YOUR BEHAVIOR

"Paying close attention to what you do changes what you do — and almost always in the right direction. You kept records of your nail-biting, did you not?"

The young man nodded.

"Did the record keeping have any effect on you?"

"Yes, I think so. It seemed that I started improving as soon as I started making tears in my little record book. I remember being intrigued by that."

"Right," said Uncle Fred. "You were monitoring your behavior, and monitoring your behavior changes your behavior. I've used this technique many, many times with excellent results, and you'll notice that self-monitoring, like modifying the environment, is extremely easy and absolutely painless. No 'will power' needed, period. Just some simple skills."

"How have you used this method?" asked the visitor.

"Years ago I had a medical problem that required me to lose some weight — and to stay slim. I remember being surrounded by friends who were using various Rambo approaches to dieting. One friend ate solid foods every other day; she was quite ornery on the diet days, and of course, she didn't keep this up for long. One friend was on a liquid diet; another paid a clinic a hefty sum for diet counseling; several just kept trying and trying — and failing and failing. Not one of them ever kept the weight off for very long. I suppose this is still fairly typical.

"Let me give you a word of advice about dieting, if I might. Don't. That's the word. Don't diet. Instead, think of ways to change the way you eat — when you eat and what you eat — and make changes that you can live with for a long, long time. If you're serious about weight and health, you need to make changes that you can live with for the rest of your life. You're better off with small changes because they're easiest to sustain.

"Can you imagine dieting for the rest of your life? What an oppressive thought. Don't diet. Manage your eating and your health-related behaviors on an ongoing basis instead. Do it — for life.

"My own weight-loss plan was simple. I modified my environment a bit and then started a weight chart. You know now about modifying the environment. Can you guess what I did?"

"Sure. You probably put a picture of a pig on your refrigerator, for one thing — lots of people do that," said the young man.

"That's an example of another self-management practice that has made its way into the public domain," said Fred. "And you're close. I put a picture of a younger, slimmer me on the refrigerator — at eye level. Where you put the picture is important, you know. A pig picture is punishing; I avoid techniques like that because they're unpleasant, and because they're unpleasant, they ultimately fail. A picture of a better me is much more encouraging than a picture of a pig. Self-management should be fun, you know.

"I also added a bathroom scale to my kitchen, and I threw away most of the fattening foods I had in the cabinets."

PERSONAL BUBBLE

One very simple change I made in my kitchen has saved me thousands of calories — and it also keeps my teeth clean! I added a toothbrush and toothpaste to the ledge above my kitchen sink. I did so because I noticed that I eat sometimes just to get a bad taste out of my mouth. Brushing my teeth works much better, and it has spared me from eating many a snack.

"But the real breakthrough," Fred continued, "was the weight chart. I posted a very simple graph in the bathroom over the scale — and of course, I attached a marker to the wall near the chart. A chart without a handy writing tool would fail in no time.

"Each morning when I awoke — the thinnest part of the day, by the way — I added a point to the graph showing my current weight. Like so." Fred sketched out his weight chart as follows:

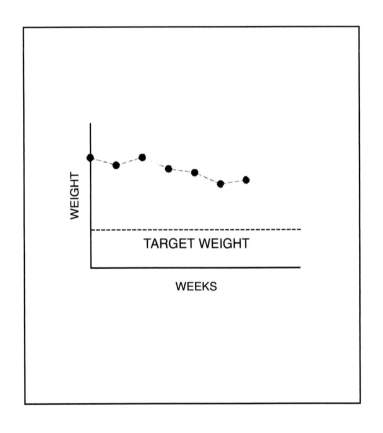

"For me," Fred continued, "this was enough. I became more aware of my weight, and that made me just a little more concerned about what I was eating. Over a period of a few months, I gradually lost the weight I needed to lose, and I've been stable ever since. I still keep the chart, but I only add a point once a week — just to make sure I never get out of hand again. Without this chart, I could very easily get off track — even now.

"I realize that a weight chart will not do the trick for everyone, but again, remember that self-management is highly personal. What I did worked for me. This is a point that I cannot overemphasize. You should not run home with one of my methods and expect it to work for you. I don't hand out fish as you know, and as you become a more proficient fisherman, you should be reluctant to take handouts. The fish you catch on your own taste the best."

"When I write," Fred said, "I always keep a chart of some sort, and charts can have many different forms. They don't have to look like conventional graphs. Remember, anything that makes you more aware of what you're doing will usually help you.

"If I have ten sections to write, I sometimes make ten little bubbles and fill them in one at a time when I complete each section. I suppose I could put gold stars on the bubbles if I had gold stars around. You can also fill in sections on a pie chart or on a thermometer — or on a snake, I guess!" Fred doodled on a piece of paper as he spoke. "There's no limit, really. Hmmm. A giraffe's neck would make a nice behavior chart, don't you think? Especially for someone who's trying to live life on a higher plane."

He smiled as he held up his doodles for the young man to see:

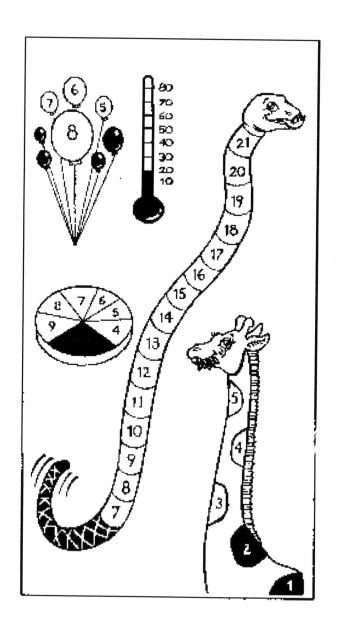

"Good charts," Fred said, "are positive and progressive. They show your target, and they show your progress. They're built to encourage you, not to depress you. They're devices for change, not accounting records. The very best ones — like the thermometer or pie chart — are cumulative. As you get closer to your goal, they get more filled up, and they never get less filled up — they never go backwards.

"As you've already discovered, charts can even be made by tearing the edge of a piece of paper. You could also throw marbles into a jar or paste stamps on a page. Any device that allows you to track your behavior will make you more aware of what you're doing, and you will very likely benefit."

"Susan told me about a fairly dramatic chart she used," said the young man. "I realize now that she was monitoring her behavior in order to change it. To stop herself from saying 'you know,' she wrote the words 'you know' on a piece of paper and attached the paper to her blouse. When she caught herself saying 'you know,' she made a tear in the paper."

"It's just like Susan to be so dramatic," said Fred. "By wearing her chart, she drew attention to her goal and thus had everyone around her heightening her awareness of the language she used. I would never go to such an extreme myself, but — as I keep saying — self-management is personal. Susan's technique worked for her.

"How long did it take her to stop saying 'you know'?"

"Just one day," said the young man.

Fred shook his head and smiled. "How very impatient young people are," he said. "What's the rush? It's we old people who should be rushing. We're the ones who are short on time."

PERSONAL BUBBLE

I've marked my progress in three different ways while writing this book. I've kept close tabs on my page count by shifting the cursor on my word processor to the bottom of my file; I've done this dozens of times. Whenever I've completed a section, I've added the starting page number to the next section in the table of contents; this has been a major thrill. And every twenty pages or so, I've printed out the entire manuscript. I've wasted paper doing so, but the rapidly thickening stack has provided especially tangible evidence that the book is getting done.

All writers use tricks of this sort, even if they are entirely unaware of the principles of self-management.

"Gizmos can be great fun," said Fred, "and they are helpful in self-monitoring. Children can monitor their behavior by moving beads on a bead bracelet, for example. Children who move a bead whenever they finish a workbook page complete more pages than children who aren't keeping track. Did you know that?"

"Not really," said the young man. "But I'm not at all surprised. Those little tears I made in my record book had an effect on me too. It was like magic."

"No, not magic. Magic's hard," said Fred. With a quick flourish, he pulled a quarter out of his right ear. "Magic takes a lot of practice. Self-management, on the other hand, is easy."

Fred threw the quarter into the air — and it was gone.

PERSONAL BUBBLE

When I first started graduate school, I wore a golf counter on my left wrist, a conventional watch on my right wrist, and a mechanical timer on my belt. I was counting and timing all sorts of behavior with much success. But my devices were too conspicuous. I noticed a student staring at me one day. I asked her what the trouble was, and she said, "What are you — a stove?"

I soon switched to less conspicuous methods of self-monitoring.

"You may have heard of self-reinforcement and self-punishment," said Fred.

"Yes, they sound familiar," said the young man, "and I think I've used self-reinforcement. I used to get myself to cut the lawn by promising myself an ice-cream sundae when I finished. Isn't that it?"

"That's the idea," said Fred, "but it's a dead-wrong idea."

"Wrong? What's wrong with it? It sounds fine to me. And I'm pretty sure it worked, too, those few times I tried it."

"Promising yourself a reward for completing a goal is indeed very helpful — but the reward isn't really rewarding anything. Its importance is in calling attention to the fact that you've met your goal. In other words, self-reinforcement and self-punishment aren't really what they seem to be. They don't really reinforce or punish anything. They're really just monitoring techniques. They mark your progress, and they heighten your awareness of what you're doing.

"Whether you choose to put a dot on a graph, a marble in a jar, or a spoonful of ice cream in your mouth — remember, monitoring what you do changes what you do, and it's almost always helpful."

"Uncle Fred," asked the young man, "does that mean monitoring can hurt sometimes?"

"I know of only one situation in which self-monitoring is disruptive, and it's not relevant to most of the day-to-day problems you're concerned about," Fred replied. "When you're performing a demanding motor task — like piano playing — heightened awareness can cause problems. If you scrutinize the movements of your fingers as they are flying over the keys, you will probably stumble. Your fingers may even get a bit tangled." Fred intertwined his fingers in a gruesome fashion and held them up with a smile.

"This probably happens because the nervous system just can't handle observing and playing at the same time. The total demand is just too great. It suggests a Heisenberg Uncertainty Principle of Behavior, if I may be so bold."

Fred grinned again. This time it was the grin of Schrödinger's cat, the very mischievous pet of a famous physicist of long ago. Fred was showing off, and he was proud of himself indeed.

"The time has come, my young friend, for your second assignment."

Fred wrote the following on a piece of paper and handed it to his guest:

SELF-MANAGEMENT
Week #2 Assignment

1. *Select a behavior to change.*
2. *Monitor that behavior.*
   Come back again next week for the third secret!
   Best of luck!

Uncle Fred

"Uncle Fred, aren't we going backwards? This assignment is shorter than last week's. I've already seen what self-monitoring can do, even though I wasn't aware of the technique."

"Last week you focused on modifying your environment," said Fred. "Recording your behavior may have helped you somewhat, but your major success came when you added the nail files. This week you'll focus on monitoring your behavior. I think you can go way beyond the kind of simple monitoring you've done so far, and you'll see that monitoring, too, can be very powerful. See how far you can take it. Throw caution to the winds!"

The young man turned to go, and then he hesitated and turned back to Fred. "Uh — Uncle Fred — do you have an idea box?" he asked.

Fred gleamed. "Yes, I do. Of course I do. Why do you ask?"

"Oh, nothing. Just a hunch," said the man. The image of a young poet was on his mind as he left to work on his new assignment.

THE

SECOND

WEEK:

EATING FOR LIFE

Even before he left Uncle Fred's home, the young man knew what he wanted to tackle. It was a tough one, but he had the confidence now to attempt it.

For years he had been concerned about his weight and his diet. As he got older, he was gaining weight gradually, and he knew his diet wasn't balanced.

When he got home, he immediately posted a weight chart over his bathroom scale. He remembered what Fred had said about the importance of a pen, so he attached a pen to the chart with some string and tape.

For the next few mornings, he weighed himself shortly after he awoke. He made sure to weigh himself before he ate breakfast — even before he brushed his teeth — to produce the most favorable numbers he could.

Unfortunately, this routine seemed to produce no effect whatsoever. His weight didn't change; if anything, he was gaining a little. And he could detect no change in his eating habits.

Nearly half the week had passed, and he felt himself getting discouraged. If it weren't for all the nail files around, he would probably have taken up nail-biting again.

Then he thought to himself, "Have I been taken in by a fish?"

After all, he had merely copied one of Uncle Fred's methods. Perhaps he was on the wrong track. He needed an approach that would work for him.

He thought, "What am I really after? What is the actual behavior I am trying to change?" Then he remembered the first item on the assignment he had received from Fred: "Select a behavior to change."

Somehow, in his haste, he had neglected to take this very simple step. He had rushed into a self-management program without being clear about what behavior he wanted to change.

He sat down with a pen and pad and thought about his behavior. He decided that he was really after several behaviors, and he wrote them down:

1. *Buy healthful foods at the supermarket.*

2. *Say no to sweets and fatty foods when offered.*

3. *Order healthful items at restaurants.*

He wasn't sure whether these behaviors would affect his weight, but they seemed like a good place to start. Even if he didn't lose weight right away, he would sure feel better about himself if he could achieve these goals.

But now what?

His second task was simply to monitor his behavior. How should he do this, and would monitoring alone have any impact?

He quickly rejected the pocket notebook procedure he had used for his nail-biting. That wouldn't work, he realized, because it wouldn't allow him to record enough information. He needed to keep track of what he ate, and even more important, he needed to know more about food so that he could make better choices.

That, he decided, was the key: more information. He headed for his local stationery store to find a good pocket diary. There he had some unexpected good luck.

A tall, slim, bright-eyed young salesperson stood behind the counter. "May I help you?" he asked.

"I'd like a pocket diary of some sort," said the young man. "And I need a little pen to go with it. And — well, a little calorie book too.
Something I could carry with the diary easily."

To the visitor's surprise, the salesperson replied, "Oh, you must be a self-manager!"

"Well, yes," said the young man. "I'm just learning self-management now. I didn't realize there were so many others around!"

"I knew it right away," said the salesperson, "when you asked for a pocket diary, a pocket pen, and a little calorie book. That combination could only mean that you are setting up a simple, portable, self-monitoring system to watch your diet. Am I right?"

"Absolutely right. Where did you learn about this?"

"My roommate in college taught me the basic principles. He got them from a psychology course. Great stuff, isn't it?"

"It's incredible!" replied the young man.

"And you're in luck," said the salesperson. He led the young man to a shelf containing various kinds of diaries. "Look," he said, picking out a small black diary. "This one has space to keep track of what you eat every day. It also comes with a small pen that's held in place by a loop. And it includes a fairly detailed list of foods, with nutrition information about each one."

"That's perfect!" said the young man. "I didn't realize that self-managers had their own products!"

"I don't think they do," said the salesperson. "But some products are perfect for self-management, even if the designers didn't have self-management in mind.

"Have you heard of the coffee maker that turns on automatically in the morning?" The young man shook his head. "It's also perfect for self-management. I had been having trouble getting up in the morning, so I bought one of these coffee makers, and I set it every night to go off just before my alarm clock does. Now I wake up every morning to the smell of freshly brewed coffee. It's great! It solved my morning blues problem completely!"

The young man bought the diary, and then at a bookstore, he bought a little book on nutrition. He recorded what he had already eaten that day, along with a count of the calories he had consumed.

As he looked up the items he had eaten, he was amazed by the numbers: The piece of fruit he had eaten at breakfast had only 37 calories, but the eggs he consumed had 285 calories, and the four pats of butter had 144! The side salad he had with his lunch had only 20 calories — but the dressing had over 300! Foods with high fat content seemed to be the culprits.

"I had no idea that calories were distributed this way — or that I was eating so foolishly," he thought.

Over the next few days, he carried his diary faithfully and looked up food calories before he ate or ordered or bought. He found himself making entirely different choices than he had his entire life, simply because he was keeping close track of what he was doing.

He also discovered that some things he had always enjoyed — pickles, cucumbers, celery, lettuce, and popcorn (without the butter!) — had a very small caloric content. Small pickles were only four calories each!

He wasn't dieting, and he wasn't trying to lose weight. He had simply heightened his awareness about the foods he bought and ate by keeping a diary.

He felt very, very good about his little diary.

PERSONAL BUBBLE

I have used a more high-tech approach to monitoring my food intake. I bought a computer program that calculated calorie-intake goals and contained nutrition information on hundreds of foods. I downloaded information on many foods into my pocket computer. Lookup is easy and fast.

It helps to know!

Over the weekend, the young man was invited to a friend's house for dinner, and there his new monitoring system caused trouble. His friend served a meat dish that he hadn't looked up yet. He panicked. The meat was an unknown. It might just as well be poison!

He excused himself to wash his hands. In the bathroom, he looked up the meat dish — and nearly dropped the diary into the toilet. "Sixteen hundred calories?" he said to himself. "That's the equivalent of 400 pickles! This is entirely unfair! I love pickles, and that meat smells awful!"

On the other hand, he didn't want to insult his host.

He returned to his seat in some distress. He picked at his food. He made small talk.

"You're not eating," said his host. "Is something wrong?"

"Well, I guess I'm not that hungry," he replied, unconvincingly.

"Are you on a diet?" asked the host.

"No, not really," he replied. "Not a diet, exactly. You see, I'm learning self — That is, I'm watching what I eat. This dish, you see —" His foot well in his mouth, he finally blurted out, "This dish has over 1600 calories."

"Does it?" replied his host. "I had no idea. Just how did you know this?"

"I looked it up while I was in your bathroom."

"I see," said the host.

There was an awkward silence.

After some delicate negotiations, the young man finally "tasted" the meat (the balance went to the dog) and had three helpings of a very delicious salad, with just a hint of dressing.

The friendship, though strained, was preserved.

When the young man went outside, he smiled suddenly and was tempted to jump and kick his heels together.

"I'm doing it!" he said aloud. "I'm in control!"

THE

THIRD

SECRET:

MAKING COMMITMENTS

"Uncle Fred, you're not going to believe this, but I'm not dieting, and I'm losing weight! I've shaved nearly 400 calories off my daily intake just by keeping track of what I'm eating. I've already lost two pounds, and I'm not even trying! And my diet is more healthful than ever.

"Look," he said, handing Fred his little black diary. "It's got its own pen and a calorie chart too. It makes it easy for me to monitor what I eat. I set three specific goals for myself, and so far I've been achieving all three."

Fred, comfortable as usual in the ragged chair, looked thoughtful as he thumbed through the diary.

"This is a very sophisticated kind of monitoring," he said. "You're keeping track of your eating and buying, and you're also looking up information about foods. You've also changed your environment by purchasing and carrying this special diary.

"You've also begun to change your body, first because you're putting different foods into it and second because you're eating less. The feeling of elation you have is coming in part from the smaller meals, I suspect. Overeating really makes you tired, don't you think?"

"Wow, does it!" said the young man.

"Are you ready for the third secret?" asked Uncle Fred.

"Shoot!"

"Once again," said Fred, "I have mis-led you a bit. You see, you've already been using the third technique — ever since you came here two weeks ago."

"What have I been doing?"

"You've been making promises," Fred answered. "You see, the third secret of self-management is to *Make Commitments*."

From one of the many cubbyholes over his desk, Fred produced the piece of paper with the two Ms on it, and then he added the words *Make Commitments*.

MODIFY YOUR ENVIRONMENT

MONITOR YOUR BEHAVIOR

MAKE COMMITMENTS

Fred handed the paper to the young man.

"You may have this now," said Fred. "It's got everything you need on it. You've heard of 'the three Rs'? Now you've got 'the three Ms,' and I think they're even more basic and more important than the Rs. Modify your environment, monitor your behavior, and make commitments. That's it! With the three Rs, you can read, write, and arith. With the three Ms, you can do anything."

"Uncle Fred," said the young man, "making commitments doesn't sound like self-management. It sounds like you're bringing other people into the picture."

"An astute comment, as usual," Fred replied. He assumed the lecture position.

"When I asked you to make promises to me two weeks ago, there was no self-management involved on your part. Technically, you were not self-managing. But say you approached me with a promise. That's quite a different story. In fact, say you approached me with a promise in order to change your own behavior in some way. Then you are definitely self-managing.

"Sometimes we need to bring other people into the picture. And when we do so on our own in order to achieve our own goals, we are the ones in control.

"Other people are necessary sometimes because of the special powers they have over us. Sometimes we need to recruit their assistance in a self-management program so that they will bring these special powers to bear.

"One special power they have is to punish or reinforce our behavior in some way — in other words, to provide consequences for our behavior. Our employers praise our accomplishments and reprimand us for our mistakes. Our spouses hug us when we've been thoughtful and shout when we've been inconsiderate.

"We can direct these kinds of powers to our own ends in a self-management program by making commitments."

"How does one do that?" asked the young man.

"Let me give you two examples from my own life," replied Fred. "One trivial, the other dramatic.

"I need to use eye drops regularly. But I hate my drops. They sting horribly, but I have been assured that they are the best ones for my condition, so I simply must make do. For a while, I used any excuse not to apply them. I was using them erratically at best, and that was doing me harm. So I put my foot down — or should I say I got steely eyed?

"I began setting the times on my wristwatch alarm clock — in other words, I modified my environment, and that was helpful. I made a chart to monitor my drops usage —"

Fred instantly produced a graph from one of the cubbyholes.

"and that was helpful," he said. "But I still wasn't entirely consistent. So I brought out the big gun — commitment.

"My daughter and her children visit my home every Sunday. Sometimes we eat a light dinner here, and sometimes we go out — which I much prefer. I told her, 'Honey, I'm still having some trouble with my drops, and I need your help. From now on, I'll show you my chart every Sunday. If I've applied the drops every time I should during the week, we can all go out to dinner to celebrate. If not, we eat in. Will you help me with this?'

"That was six months ago, and I've only missed my drops twice since then. I hate my drops, but I hate eating in even more."

"I'm a little confused," said the young man. "What exactly did you commit to, and what role did your daughter play?"

"Good questions!" Fred replied. "I made a commitment both to myself and to my daughter to take my drops. And then I added the extra — and essential ingredient in a commitment procedure: I asked my daughter to be an enforcer. It's her job to reinforce my good behavior or punish my bad behavior — because I've asked her to, and I've even told her what to do.

"Notice the difference between acommitment procedure and the proverbial New Year's resolution. A New Year's resolution is made to yourself only. You haven't brought anyone else in on it, so there's no one to enforce it — no one to provide consequences for your behavior.

"In a commitment procedure, you are recruiting a friend or family member to enforce your commitment. You are asking another person to provide consequences for your behavior. This is a very powerful approach to self-management, but, of course, it's not as private as the other two methods, and it's more stressful. It also depends on the good faith of the enforcer. You need to pick someone you trust.

"If the other techniques fail, keep commitment in mind as a supplement to them. It's especially helpful when you need to get yourself to do something that goes against the grain — like using those drops!"

Fred grimaced.

"I got myself to study calculus in college by joining a study group," said the young man. "I knew that once I told my friends I was coming, I would probably show up. Is that an example of a commitment procedure?"

"Most definitely," said Uncle Fred.

"And a girlfriend of mine used to schedule appointments that overlapped with the dinner hour in our cafeteria. She did it deliberately so that she'd arrive at the cafeteria at the last minute so she wouldn't have time for second helpings. It was how she controlled her eating."

"Another good example," said Fred. "Some people schedule early morning appointments so that they will get up earlier and have more productive days. It's the same idea.

"And I'm calling your attention to the most general case: You can use commitment procedures to change your behavior in any number of ways. It's a powerful procedure, and it can be very helpful."

PERSONAL BUBBLE

In college I got myself to run every day by arranging to do so with my friend Douglas. Unfortunately, the system broke down one day when Douglas wanted a day off and I got angry. We had made mutual commitments to run every day, and when he broke his commitment, he got punished. But so did I! That's the risk we take when the commitments are mutual, as in marriage. Both parties have to stay committed, or the relationship breaks down.

"This brings me to my second example," said Fred. "And it's rather personal. Come, we need to go upstairs for this story."

Fred led his guest to the fireplace in the living room. On the mantle was a ceramic sculpture of a man on a horse. Fred placed his hand on the sculpture.

"This is my most prized possession," he said. "It's a sculpture of me, made more than fifty years ago by a dear friend. He died of cancer shortly after he made the piece.

"My family always called it the 'Quiet Dad.' Can you guess why?"

Fred had a faraway look in his eyes. There was no sign of a grin.

"No," said the young man. "You don't look very peaceful on the horse. You even look a little angry."

"Very perceptive," Fred said. "As a younger man, I was pretty intense — highstrung, I guess you could say. I was easily angered.

"Like many parents, I lost control of myself and yelled at my children sometimes, usually over nothing. One day I yelled at my three-year-old daughter, and she got so scared that she ran in that direction —"

Fred stretched his arm toward the door to the basement stairs.

"without looking. She fell down the stairs, all the way to the bottom.

"She wasn't hurt. It was amazing. She was crying, but she was barely even bruised. When she was calm, I called everyone together in this room, and I said, 'If I ever raise my voice to any of you again, I want you to smash this sculpture.' And I never, ever raised my voice to my wife or children again."

When they resumed their meeting in Fred's study, the young man admitted that he had had some trouble with his weight loss routine when he first started out.

"I was using a fish, Uncle Fred. I just copied what you did rather than thinking the problem through."

"There are two lessons in that," Fred replied. "The first is to beware of fish. That you learned. The second lesson is to keep trying. When one technique fails, try another, or try several at once. Remember, you are in control, and your new skills can go a long, long way. I've never found a problem I can't beat. The skills are that powerful."

"I also had some trouble," said the young man, "when I tried to talk to other people about my new program. I had a very embarrassing dinner as a result."

"Set up a program that's right for you. If you devise a program that's public in some way — like Susan's 'you know' sign — be sure you can handle it! If you need a program that's entirely private, make it private!

"As a self-manager, you have unlimited flexibility. No one's looking over your shoulder. If a technique isn't working quite right, you can tinker with it. If you want to go back to one you used last year, do it. No one will ever know.

"Managers of other people don't have this kind of leeway. Their staff members and superiors would lose confidence in them if they fiddled constantly with their policies and procedures. They can't be completely responsive to the effects of their decisions; they often have to make a decision and run with it, no matter what the consequences.

"Self-managers don't have constraints of that sort. As a self-manager, you're your own boss, and you have just one employee. You can be wholly responsive to that employee because that employee is you."

"You're amply ready now for your third and last assignment," said Uncle Fred. He wrote the following on a piece of paper and handed it to the young man.

SELF-MANAGEMENT
Week #3 Assignment

1. *Select a behavior to change.*
2. *Make a commitment to change, and give a friend the power to oversee your commitment.*
   Best of luck, always!

Uncle Fred

"I'll do it, Uncle Fred, and I will succeed," said the young man.

As the young man prepared to leave the study, he said to Fred, "Oh, I almost forgot. I've brought you something."

He reached into a pocket of his overcoat and produced a glistening red apple.

As he placed it on Fred's desk, he said, "And I need to tell you something very important about this apple."

He paused for dramatic effect.

"This apple has 81 calories and 0.5 grams of fat!"

They both laughed heartily.

"By the way, Uncle Fred," said the young man, "could I possibly come see you again next week, just to let you know how I'm progressing?"

"Of course," said Fred, the mischievous grin appearing suddenly.

"Could we make a firm appointment?"

"Absolutely," said Fred. "I see you're getting the point. You're making a commitment, aren't you? Did you do this in order to make sure you'd follow through with your new self-management plan?"

The young man nodded.

"Then you are a self-manager. I'll see you same time next week."

SELF-HELP WITHOUT THE HYPE

THE

THIRD

WEEK:

NO MORE SMOKING

Even before the young man reached his home, he had selected his third target behavior and a simple commitment plan. He smoked a cigarette in the car, knowing that it would be one of the last cigarettes he'd ever smoke.

At home he wrote checks to every controversial political organization and religious sect he could think of. For good measure, he wrote a letter to his boss telling him off in graphic language. He put them all in stamped envelopes addressed to the relevant parties.

Then he called his sister on the telephone. She was an ideal enforcer, he realized, because he and she had always been close and because she had been trying to get him to stop smoking for years.

"I'm quitting smoking as of midnight tonight," he told her. "And I need your help to make sure I don't start again. Will you help me?"

"Of course," his sister replied, "but what can I do?"

"I'm coming by with some letters. If I ever start smoking again, I want you to mail them all — no matter what I do, no matter how hard I protest. And if I ask you to return them to me, say no!"

"Are you serious about this?" she asked.

"Dead serious," her brother replied. "Smoking is a life-and-death matter for me. I hate what it does to my health and my breath, and I resent spending so much money on it. You know I've tried quitting before, and I've never quite made it. I need this extra boost to make sure I quit for good."

"But aren't you putting yourself under my control? Shouldn't you be quitting on your own?" she asked.

"No, I'm the one in control here. I've made the decision to quit, and I'm simply enlisting your help. You get nothing out of this program — except some additional responsibility in your life. I'm the one who gains. And I'll be grateful to you forever for your help."

"I'll do what you ask, of course," she replied.

The young man delivered the letters to his sister. He trembled as he handed them to her, and he felt enormously relieved when they were no longer in his hand. He felt unburdened, free. This is how Uncle Fred must have felt, the young man thought, when he offered up his sculpture to his family members. It was a great feeling.

He had brought all his cigarettes and lighters to his sister's home. They sang "Auld Lang Syne" over the trash can in the garage as the disposed of the lot.

On his way home he picked up an "I Quit for Good" button from a local pharmacy. "This is one change that's going to be public," he said to himself. "I want everyone to know about me. I deserve some congratulations!"

When he emerged from his car, he ran, leaped into the air, and kicked his heels together. He'd been wanting to for days, after all.

THE

FOURTH

VISIT:

THE SELF-MANAGEMENT PRINCIPLE

"Nice button," said Fred, smiling broadly.

"Uncle Fred," said the young man, "I quit smoking in one day with a simple commitment procedure. And I'll never smoke again. I'm not even tempted."

"I told you self-management is easy, and it is," Fred replied. "It's just a matter of developing the right skills. Good management involves a set of skills that people can learn, and good self-management also involves skills that people can learn. That's all there is to it.

"How is your eating program going?"

"I'm down four pounds, and I'm not dieting. I'm just keeping my food diary. And it's gotten faster and easier for me to keep the diary, because I only need to look up a food if I'm unfamiliar with it. I've got six different kinds of pickles in my refrigerator, and I've become a real connoisseur of sparkling water. If anything, I'm eating far more than I used to, and I never feel hungry. But now I'm making informed decisions about what I eat.

"I'm also beginning to think about some simple procedures that will make it easy and natural for me to exercise more. And I've got some good ideas about how to get better organized at work. A few months from now, Uncle Fred, you won't recognize me — mainly because I'll have a permanent smile on my face — like you do!"

"All well and good," Fred replied, "all well and good. But you still have a great deal to learn about self-management."

"I do?"

"Oh, yes," said Fred. "Are you ready for an advanced lesson?"

"Absolutely," said the young man.

The lecture began.

"Do you know why televisions work?" asked Uncle Fred.

"No, not at all," said the young man.

"Very few people do, I'm sure," said Fred. "You know how to use the TV, and that's enough. You don't really need to know how or why a TV works.

"Self-management is similar. You now have the basic skills. You know how to do it, and that may be enough. But would you be interested in knowing something about why these skills work?"

"Sure!" said the young man.

"Okay, then," said Fred, "hang on to your seat.

"In everyday life, most people learn a small handful of self-management tricks — like setting an alarm clock. You, on the other hand, have learned three general self-management skills: Modify Your Environment, Monitor Your Behavior, and Make Commitments. These skills will allow you to develop thousands of self-management programs of your own to suit almost any situation.

"Above and beyond these skills is a general principle called The Self-Management Principle. The three skills are just applications of this one general principle.

"Here is the principle." A large white piece of paper materialized from above Fred's desk, and on it he wrote the following:

"Behavior Changes Behavior."

BEHAVIOR CHANGES BEHAVIOR

"Behavior changes behavior. In other words, when you do one thing, that changes the likelihood that you'll do something else. When you walk by a restaurant, that increases the likelihood that you'll eat. When you take deep breaths, that decreases the likelihood that you'll argue with someone. When you set an alarm clock, that increases the likelihood that you'll get up early the next morning. When you keep a record of the foods you eat, that increases the likelihood that you'll eat more healthful foods. One behavior affects another. Do you get the idea?"

"Yes, I think so," replied the young man. "Different behaviors are connected. The hip behavior is connected to the thigh behavior, so to speak." "Exactly," said Fred, grinning. "Now this principle applies to everyone, everyday, but most people don't know about it or don't think about it. Self-managers, on the other hand, utilize this principle to help them. They take advantage of this simple principle. They make it work for them.

"For example, fructose — a sugar found in many fruits — suppresses the appetite. Someone who is not skilled in self-management might, from time to time, eat an apple shortly before dinner. As a result, he or she will eat substantially less for dinner, even taking the apple into account.

"A self-manager, on the other hand, will deliberately eat an apple or a pear every night before dinner — in order to suppress the appetite. Do you see the difference?"

"Sure, I see," replied the young man. "When I set up this appointment with you, I did so deliberately in order to change my own behavior — in order to increase the likelihood that I would follow through on my third assignment. Is that it?"

"Bull's-eye," said Fred, emphatically. "Self-managers are always asking themselves what they can do in order to change the likelihood of some other behavior. It's that simple. When you modify your environment as part of a self-management program, you are engaging in one behavior in order to change another. When you monitor yourself as part of a self-management program, you are engaging in one behavior in order to change another. When you make a commitment as part of a self-management program, you are engaging in one behavior in order to change another.

"You may also do any of these things for other reasons. If you move your desk to the other side of the room in order to make the room look nicer, you are not self-managing — you are redecorating. You self-manage when you take advantage of The Self-Management Principle — that is, when you deliberately engage in one behavior in order to change another.

"With this principle, the world of self-management is yours."

"Have you ever thought about why people need to self-manage?" asked Uncle Fred.

"No," said the young man. "But I guess some of us just get out of control otherwise."

"Right," said Fred, "and if you'll be patient with me for the next few minutes, I'll explain why this is so. Remember when we talked about reinforcers on a previous visit?"

"Sure," said the young man. "Reinforcers are things we like, right?"

"That's very close," Fred replied. "To be more precise, a reinforcer is something you would normally work to attain, like money or food or praise. When your behavior is reinforced, that usually feels pretty good, and in general, reinforcers are pretty good. But some reinforcers are peculiar. They're like wolves in sheep's clothing. They're not what they seem to be. I guess you could call them dark reinforcers."

"How can that be?" asked the young man.

"Presumably for genetic reasons, one of my children has always been far more impulsive than the other. You could see it in the way they ate chocolate chip cookies as young children. The impulsive child always ate each cookie from one end to the other The prudent child always ate around the chocolate chips, saving the best part for the very last bite.

"So, to answer the question: People get out of control because the world is full of dark reinforcers — reinforcers that are connected to delayed punishment. It can be awfully hard to resist such reinforcers.

"Self-management techniques make it easy for all of us to have self-control. They make it easy for all of us to avoid dark reinforcers. We need self-management techniques for the simple reason that rein-forcers are not always benign.

"End of technical lecture!"

Fred grinned again, immensely pleased with the speech he had given — like a child taking a curtain call at the end of a Christmas play, thought the young man.

"You are a remarkable person, Uncle Fred," he said.

"Thanks," said Fred, still beaming. He had worked hard for that reinforcer, it seemed.

"Because some reinforcers — the dark ones — are connected to punishers — consequences you would normally work hard to avoid, like reprimands or taxes or electric shocks. When your behavior is punished, that usually feels bad. Dark reinforcers are tied to punishers, and usually the punishers are long–delayed.

"For example, a piece of chocolate cake is a reinforcer, but it's a dark reinforcer because it's tied to many delayed punishers: weight gain, blood sugar problems, cardiovascular problems, even relationship problems. Unprotected sexual intercourse is a powerful reinforcer, but it, too, is dark because it's connected to many possible punishers: unwanted pregnancy, sexually transmitted diseases, and so on. Alcohol and drugs are also powerful reinforcers, but they, too, are tied to powerful delayed punishers — serious health problems, car accidents, relationship problems, and so on.

"Dark reinforcers of this type are usually called temptations. When you hear the word temptation, look hard and you will find a reinforcer that's connected to delayed punishment: adultery, petty thievery, drug smuggling — every forbidden activity you can think of — every temptation ever invented — involves immediate reinforcement and delayed punishment.

"When faced with a reinforcer — when that chocolate cake is right in front of you — the tendency is to go for it, even if it is connected to punishment. In other words, dark reinforcers are still reinforcers. They're just reinforcers that can cause trouble for us later. Our parents, our spiritual leaders, our teachers, and our governments pinpoint many of these peculiar reinforcers for us and urge us to avoid them — to resist temptation. The Surgeon General put a dark reinforcer warning on every pack of cigarettes and every cigarette ad. We are urged to stay away from certain foods or certain people, to avoid drugs or alcohol, to refrain from sex or engage in safe sex.

"People who stay clear of most dark reinforcers with little effort or who push them aside easily are greatly admired. We say they show self-control. People who have trouble resisting dark reinforcers are often called impulsive.

"Let's talk about daily strategy," said
Fred. "Self-management, like any other
skill, requires practice. The more you practice, the better you'll be.

"Self-management should be prac-
ticed daily, even when nothing seems to be
wrong in your life. The fact is, you can
always improve yourself, no matter how
good things are going."

"Do you practice self-management
every day?" asked the young man.

"Most certainly. It's practically a reli-
gion with me," answered Uncle Fred. "I
spend a minute each morning — I call it
my Morning Minute — thinking about
areas I might like to work on. It's a very
rare morning that I can't think of some
area that needs work.

"This morning, for example, I thought
about exercising. I'm getting a bit shaky
on my exercise bike — my balance is going
with my vision, I'm afraid. It occurred to
me that a pleasant alternative might be a
morning walk. I could make walking fairly
easy and natural by a simple change in my
environment: I could cancel my newspaper
subscription! There's a newspaper dis-
penser about three blocks away. I could
see myself very happily taking a walk each
day to get a newspaper.

"The point is this: Spend a little time each day — a Morning Minute, if that suits your needs — thinking about your life. Don't just live your life, manage it! Reflect on it and make it better.

"This should be a lifelong practice because there is always a need for self-management. Circumstances change and bring new problems and new challenges. You get a new girlfriend or a new boss or a new job. Your body changes — and eventually deteriorates. You need to stay one jump ahead! Otherwise you may as well pack up and die.

"Personally," Fred continued, "I'd like to die like a pigeon. They never grow old, you know. They show hardly any signs of aging. One day they just keel over. Bam, they're dead. Alive and fully functioning one minute, gone the next. That's what I want."

"Shall we talk about creativity?" asked Fred.

"Yes, please," replied the young man. "Look," said Fred.

He opened the large lower-left drawer of his desk — the one you usually use for file folders. But instead of folders, it contained hundreds of pieces of paper of all sizes and shapes.

"This is my idea box," said Fred, "or, more precisely, my idea drawer. It's a kind of way station for ideas.

"We're all creative, in the sense that we all have interesting and novel ideas pop into our heads all the time. But very few of us have developed the skills to capture those ideas — to pay attention to them, first of all, and then to freeze them in some form so we can follow up on them later."

"A little girl in Susan's classroom told me that ideas were like rabbits," said the young man, "and that they run by so fast that we are lucky to see their ears and tails. She, too, said you had to capture them. I was moved to see such a beautiful image coming from a child."

"Then you have forgotten your child-hood!" said Fred. "Children are experts at being creative. They pay close attention to every new idea they have, and they try very hard to act on each one. Unfortunately, we soon discourage them from doing this. Much is lost when people are socialized, as I'm sure you know.

"Fortunately, you can use your self-management skills to get the ball rolling once more. Simply find conditions under which you pay attention to your novel thoughts, and then make arrangements to capture your ideas. Have you heard of the Three Bs of Creativity?" The young man shook his head. "Well, for some people, the Bed, the Bath, and the Bus are good places for paying attention to novel ideas. But you must find your own special places and your own ideal conditions.

"In the summer, I have good luck sit-ting alone by the pool in my back yard. I keep a notebook and pen right at hand, of course. Good ideas disappear quickly! And you already discovered the tape recorder by my bed.

"I also have good luck with large white pieces of paper." Fred withdrew one from the idea drawer. "I just sit quietly sometimes at my desk and jot down whatever words or images come to me. Usually I get nonsense. Sometimes I get brilliant ideas — very few of which, unfortunately, I can act upon.

"Hmmm," he said, looking at the sheet in front of him, "here I seem to have an idea for ending the energy crisis. Sorry — can't let you see it," he said, grinning, and tossed it back into the drawer.

"My ideas," said Fred, "go from my notebooks or tape recorder to this drawer and from here to my cubbyholes or file folders. This system works for me. If you want to enhance your own creativity, use your self-management skills to develop a system that works for you."

"I know, Uncle Fred," the young man exclaimed, "no fish!"

"I still have one worry at this point, Uncle Fred," the young man said. "Will I be able to keep a program going for a long time? Controlling my diet means a lifetime program — or at least I hope so."

"This is called the 'maintenance' problem," Fred replied. "And maintenance is an issue in its own right. Look at it this way: If you're concerned about long-term maintenance, plan for it. Use your skills to develop strategies to keep yourself on a program for a long period of time.

"I used to monitor my weight every day, as you know. Now I just weigh myself once a week. I adjusted my program to make it easy for me to stick with it for the long haul — over twenty years in this case.

"You can also make long-term commitments: You may have heard about the television personality who lost a lot of weight and then announced publicly that she would keep the weight off for a year. She failed, of course, because she had lost the weight through a crash diet; she had never learned self-management skills, so she simply gained the weight back, as most people do. Later, she learned some self-management skills, and she's stayed fairly slim since then.

"If you're concerned about the long term, consider making small changes. Go for changes that you know you can live with for a long, long time.

"As a self-manager, you can make changes, and you can maintain changes. Period."

"Do the Three Ms cover all self-management techniques, Uncle Fred?"

"All self-management techniques," Fred replied, "are covered by The Self-Management Principle: Behavior Changes Behavior. The Three Ms are broad categories of skills that make use of this principle, but no, they don't include all self-management techniques. Remember the overriding principle, and you may find yourself with a program someday that doesn't fit the Three Ms.

"And stay alert to people around you who may be able to teach you even more about self-management. Even people who aren't self-managers can do this sometimes. Remember, some people have picked up effective self-management techniques without formal training. Look for them, and you will find them!

"But remember, too, that the general skills are far more valuable than any particular application. Don't borrow too many fish! Keep practicing your fishing, instead! Then you will never go hungry."

"Now," said Uncle Fred, "if you don't mind, we need to end our meeting. I'm getting a bit tired."

Fred stood up a bit unsteadily.
"You'll keep in touch, won't you?" he asked.

The young man choked up suddenly. His training was truly over now, and he didn't want it to end — and he treasured his contact with Uncle Fred.

He took a breath.

"Sure, Uncle Fred," he replied, getting to his feet. "Of course I will."

"Well, then. Carry on." And Fred extended his arm, offering his hand for the young man to shake.

ANOTHER

CHAT

WITH

SUSAN

Images of child self-managers kept running through the young man's mind — especially that of the little poet. He found himself thinking about Susan, the young teacher, and he finally called her.

"I really enjoyed talking to you the other day," he said. "And I think what you've done with your students is amazing. I really admire you."

"It sounds like you want me just for my self-management skills," Susan quipped.

They met at a café over two bottles of imported sparkling water — hers with a twist of lime, his with a twist of lemon. He didn't need to look this one up: Water has no calories at all!

"Are you sure you want to see me?" she asked. "I'm liable to talk your ear off at times."

"That's okay," he replied. "I know you're working on it. And I'm not perfect, either, you know. Whoops! I just said you know, didn't I?"

"Don't worry!" Susan exclaimed. "I've got a great program for that!"

"No way!" said the young man. "I'm not going around with a piece of paper on my shirt. I'll make my own program! I'm a self-manager, and I don't take fish!"

They both laughed at the joke only they — and maybe a few others — could understand.

EPILOGUE

Three months had passed since the young man's fourth meeting with Uncle Fred.

And with each new day came new success and new joy. The young man sharpened his skills with practice, and when one approach failed, he tried another. He tackled every challenge optimistically and with the confidence that comes of skill and experience.

He exercised regularly and ate properly. He stopped smoking. He slept soundly and awoke easily. He was more patient in relationships. He was better organized. He began assignments early and completed them on time. He began an idea jar. His fingernails were the envy of his office mates.

When leaving a friend's house one day, he noticed a sign posted on the inside of the back door. It read, "Remember to Turn Off the Lights Before You Leave!"

The young man turned to his friend and said, "Oh, I see you're a self-manager."

"A what?" said the friend.

"A self-manager. Self-managers do things to change the likelihood they'll do other things. You put up this sign because you had been forgetting to turn your lights off, and you wanted to change your behavior."

"Yes, that's right," said the friend. "That's why I put up the sign, but I never thought about it in general terms."

"What you did," said the young man, "exemplifies a general principle — The Self-Management Principle — and it's well worth learning. There are also three simple secrets that go along with the principle. Learning them changed my life completely just a few months ago."

"Really? Would you be willing to teach me about them?" asked the friend.

"Sure," the young man replied, "in fact, I'm committed to helping you."

"What?"

"Private joke," he said. "I'll explain during our first training session."

His friend still looked puzzled.

"Don't worry," said the young man. "I'll teach you to be a great self-manager. It's easy when you know how. Believe me, if I could learn it, anyone can. And you're already ahead of where I was when I started. Have a free afternoon next week?"

They set a meeting time.

The secrets were revealed.

And a new self-manager was born.

ONE FINAL BUBBLE

Remember to beware of fish!

This book gives many examples of how some fictitious characters and I have used self-management skills to solve our problems and shape our lives. If you feel that these examples are appropriate to your life, feel free to try the particular methods that have been described.

But this book will have far greater value in your life if you practice the three general skills of self-management, rather than copying any of the particular applications.

Modify Your Environment, Monitor Your Behavior, and Make Commitments. How you do so is up to you, and if one method fails, try another, or try several at once. Remember, self-change is easy when you have the right skills.

Good fishing, and good living!

Robert Epstein

SAY NO TO FISH!

LOOK OUT!

ACKNOWLEDGMENTS

Two good friends of mine who have never met — Lyle M. Spencer, Jr. and Dennis S. Thompson — suggested that I write this book, and for that I am grateful. Both knew about my long-standing interest in self-control and self-management, and both have background in business and the behavioral sciences. They each suggested the same approach, and at one point, they even suggested the same title.

I guess Susan's Uncle Mort was right: "Great minds think alike, and —" Well, at least Uncle Mort was half right.

I am also grateful to Lyle and Signe Spencer for providing the ideal space for me in which to write a draft of this book and to Karen Searles Brethower for support, encouragement, and timely advice. Sandra Katz, a professor of English, made valuable corrections to the text.

I am especially grateful to B. F. Skinner for sharing five years of his life with me and allowing me an intimate look at a master self-manager at work. I had been studying and practicing self-management for years before I met Fred Skinner, but I had never seen anyone so good at it. He was a most remarkable man.

It would take another book this size to reveal the extent to which the fictional character Uncle Fred and the real Fred Skinner overlapped. I will spare the reader this exercise, except for a few tidbits: FredSkinner really did sleep in his basement study for many years, in large part to enhance his productivity, and he really kept a tape recorder by his bed. He really did contour his seat cushion at one point, but he eventually replaced the chair because it was unsightly. (Social norms can compete with good self-management, just as "Uncle Fred" said.) He really charted his behavior to good effect, and he really had idea folders (but not an idea box). He did not subscribe to a tri-partite secrets plan, but he certainly believed that self-management was within every person's grasp.

Fred did not say he wanted to "die like a pigeon," but there is more than a grain of truth in what I wrote. Pigeons do indeed show few signs of aging. They live long lives, and they die rather suddenly — fully functioning one minute, dead the next. Fred Skinner left this world with much the same energy in August, 1990 at age 86. He accepted the first Lifetime Achievement Award of the American Psychological Association a week before his death, and he put the finishing touches on a major essay just hours before the end. He lived by his wits, happily and fully, and he died with his wits.

And so might we all.

ABOUT THE AUTHOR

Robert Epstein received his Ph.D. in psychology from Harvard University in 1981. He has published more than 75 scholarly and scientific articles in journals such as *Science, Nature,* and the *Proceedings of the National Academy of Sciences,* and is the author of *Generativity Theory,* a scientific theory of creativity. His research on creativity and problem solving has been reported in *Time* magazine, the *New York Times, Discover,* and elsewhere.

His recent books include *Irrelativity* (Astrion, 1997), *Creativity Games for Trainers* (McGraw-Hill, 1996) and *Cognition, Creativity, and Behavior: Selected Essays* (Praeger, 1996). He is also the editor of two books of the writings of the late Professor B. F. Skinner.

Epstein is the founder and Director Emeritus of the Cambridge Center for Behavioral Studies in Massachusetts and has taught at Boston University, Simmons College, the University of Massachusetts at Amherst, Keio University (Tokyo), the University of California San Diego, the HAL Institute of Computer Technology (Osaka), and other universities; his laboratory is located at the Center for Behavioral Epidemiology at San Diego State University.

Epstein's popular writings have appeared in *Reader's Digest, Parenting, The Washington Post, Psychology Today,* and other magazines and newspapers, and his commentaries on AIDS, behavioral medicine, and other topics have aired worldwide on the Voice of America and National Public Radio. He is a contributing editor for *Psychology Today* magazine, and he has done training and consulting for major corporations and psychiatric facilities since 1982.

Epstein recently served as National University's first Research Professor and was previously Professor of Psychology and Chair of the psychology department there. His newest book is *Pure Fitness: Body Meets Mind,* co-authored with Lori "Ice" Fetrick of TV's "American Gladiators" (Masters Press), and his book *Stress-Management and Relaxation Games for Trainers* will appear soon. Epstein is now at work on a series of children's books that teach traditional values. He can be reached by e-mail at epstein@juno.com or by fax at 760-436-4490.

Give a man a fish,
and he will not be hungry.

Teach a man to fish,
and he will *never* be hungry.

—The Talmud

SELF-HELP WITHOUT THE HYPE